Theodore Roosevelt and the Dakota Badlands

by Chester L. Brooks and Ray H. Mattison

Published by Theodore Roosevelt Nature & History Association
201 East River Road North, PO Box 167
Medora, ND 58645
701-623-4884

Front Cover Photograph:
Theodore Roosevelt in 1885.
Library of Congress LC-DIG-ppmsca-35995

ISBN: 978-1-7365905-1-5

Printed by the National Park Service in 1958 & 1962

Reprinted with revisions by
Theodore Roosevelt Nature & History Association
1983 and 2008

Reprinted with revisions by
Theodore Roosevelt Nature and History Association
Layout and Design by Jesse Sexton
2022

Contents

Preface i
Acknowledgments iv
The North Dakota Badlands 1
Early History of the Badlands 2
    Fur Traders and Travelers. 2
    The Indian Wars 3
    The Coming of the Railroad. 4
    The Open Range Cattle Industry 7
Town of Little Missouri 9
Little Missouri and Medora 11
Lawlessness in the Little Missouri Region 11
Roosevelt the Buffalo Hunter 14
Roosevelt Buys a Cattle Ranch 16
A Typical Cattle Drive 19
Roosevelt the Rancher 21
Roosevelt and the Marquis de Mores 29
The Stockmen's Association 31
The Winter of 1886-87 33
Roosevelt's Later Ranching Operations 37
The Further Career of the Marquis de Mores 38
Roosevelt's Later Visits to Medora 39
Roosevelt and the Conservation Movement 40
Establishment of the Park 42

Preface

Theodore Roosevelt National Park was established to commemorate the enduring contributions of Theodore Roosevelt in the conservation of our Nation's resources and to portray his part in developing the northern open range cattle industry, a phase of history in which he was an enthusiastic participant. While in the Badlands he witnessed the passing of one of the last frontiers of the West. In 1888 he wrote, "Up to 1880 the country through which the Little Missouri flows remained as wild and almost as unknown as it was when old explorers and fur traders crossed it in the early part of the century."

Although Theodore Roosevelt was not an unknown public figure when he first came to the Little Missouri region in September 1883, the facts about some of his ventures there are obscure. It is known that he visited the Little Missouri Badlands frequently until 1886, less often thereafter. The contemporary evidences we have concerning him during his sporadic visits are to be found in the incomplete files of several newspapers, Roosevelt's letters to his family and a few intimate friends, the tax records of Billings and Stark Counties, and the books in which he wrote about his experiences there as a hunter and a rancher.

Roosevelt was born on October 27, 1858, at 28 East 20th Street, New York City. His family was well-to-do. As a child, he was delicate, suffering from cholera morbus, and an asthmatic condition. To overcome his physical handicaps, he early developed a fondness for sports and an interest in natural history. Roosevelt graduated from Harvard in 1880 with a developed interest in history, natural history, and writing which he maintained throughout his life.

Theodore Roosevelt, New York Assemblyman, 1884.
Library of Congress, LC-DIG-ppmsca-37557

"My home ranch-house stands on the river brink. From the low, long veranda, shaded by leafy cotton-woods, one looks across sand bars and shallows to a strip of meadowland, behind which rises a line of sheer cliffs and grassy plateaus. This veranda is a pleasant place in the summer evenings when a cool breeze stirs along the river and blows in the faces of the tired men, who loll back in their rocking-chairs (what true American does not enjoy a rocking-chair?), book in hand--though they do not often read the books, but rock gently to and fro, gazing sleepily out at the weird-looking buttes opposite, until their sharp outlines grow indistinct and purple in the after-glow of the sunset."

- Theodore Roosevelt -

Acknowledgments

This new edition would not be possible without the help of many individuals. First and foremost a thanks to former National Park Service historians Chester Brooks and Ray Mattison who authored most of this text.

Thanks to the staff at Theodore Roosevelt Nature and History Association for publishing this book. Jesse Sexton for undertaking this new edition from tracking down archival photographs and permissions to the formatting of this new project. Tracy Sexton for supporting the printing of this publication and other publications, which offer National Park Visitors the opportunity to continue to learn about the history of western North Dakota.

Thanks to the knowledgeable and responsive staff of the Theodore Roosevelt Center at Dickinson State University, particularly Sharon Kilzer and Erik Johnson.

Thanks to Sarah Walker of the North Dakota State Archives, Heather Hultman and Jeff Malcomson of the Montana Historical Society, and Christine Jacobson of the Houghton Library at Harvard University who promptly and with great effort provided resources and photographs for this project.

The North Dakota Badlands

This region which Theodore Roosevelt knew appears to have sunk away from the surrounding world. The panorama of colorful buttes and mesas, washes, and sharply eroded valleys was carved by the Little Missouri River and its tributaries. From its source in western Wyoming the Little Missouri River winds in a northerly direction through the southeastern corner of Montana and the northwestern corner of South Dakota to join the Missouri River in west-central North Dakota.

A typical badlands scene.
Theodore Roosevelt Nature & History Association/Ashley Griffin

Before the Ice Age, the waters of the Little Missouri, through the Yellowstone and Missouri Rivers, emptied into Hudson Bay. During the advance of the continental glacier the outlet of the Little Missouri was blocked by the advancing ice, which diverted its course east to join the Missouri River near Fort Berthold. The elevation of its new mouth was considerably lower than where it had joined the Yellowstone east of Williston. The resulting down-cutting of the river and its tributaries in a soil and rock cover easily susceptible to erosion contributed to the formation of the badlands topography.

This arresting topography is the result of geological processes operating over millions of years. The surface rocks were laid down

40 to 60 million years ago. At that time streams originating in the newly uplifted Rocky Mountains flowed eastward and deposited their sediments in lagoons, lakes, and deltas that existed then. In time, these layers of sediment were changed to rock strata, which were later uplifted and are now found over a large part of western North Dakota and eastern Montana. The vegetation which flourished then was covered with sediments and later converted by tremendous pressures and other forces into lignite coal. Through the burning of the lignite, some of the upper clay beds were baked into a red brick-like rock, known locally as "scoria," which now caps many of the buttes.

Early History of the Badlands

Surprisingly little is known about the occupation or use by Indians of the Little Missouri Badlands prior to travel by white men and their settlement in the region. During the 19th century, Crow, Cheyenne, Sioux, Arikara, Mandan, and Gros Ventre Indians variously occupied sites along the Missouri River above Bismarck, from the mouth of the Knife River to the mouth of the Yellowstone. The area drained by the Little Missouri, the largest tributary of the Missouri in this region, was frequented by these tribes for hunting and camping.

Fur Traders and Travelers

It was probably not until about 1804 that white men first viewed the Little Missouri Badlands. That year Jean Baptiste LePage, a Canadian "voyageur," descended the Little Missouri River and joined the Lewis and Clark Expedition at its winter camp at Fort Mandan north of Bismarck. During the next two decades many trapping and exploring expeditions, notably those of John Colter, Manuel Lisa, Joshua Pilcher, Alexander Henry, William Sublette, William Kipp, and Brig. Gen. Henry Atkinson passed the mouth of the Little Missouri River en route to the Yellowstone River or the Three Forks region. Doubtless the upper reaches of the Little Missouri were explored by trappers or hunters attached to these expeditions, but no definite record of their wanderings survives.

Kipp's trading post, at the mouth of White Earth River, below present Williston, built in 1826, was the white habitation nearest to the

Badlands. With the inauguration of steamboat travel on the Missouri in 1832 to Fort Union, an American Fur Company trading post near the present Montana-North Dakota boundary, a succession of fur traders, adventurers, artists, and scientists passed the mouth of the Little Missouri. Among the more distinguished travelers were Prince Maximilian of Wied, Carl Bodmer, Father Pierre de Smet, George Catlin, Kenneth McKenzie, John James Audubon, and Pierre Chouteau.

In 1845, the American Fur Company erected Fort Berthold at Like-a-Fishhook Village, stronghold of the Arikara, Gros Ventre, and Mandan Indians, about 15 miles below the mouth of the Little Missouri. These settlements, coupled with a growing traffic along the Missouri River, would make it seem probable that the Little Missouri wilderness was penetrated frequently by hunting or exploring parties.

The Indian Wars

The Little Missouri River region was first brought to the attention of the American people through the campaign of Brig. Gen. Alfred Sully against the Sioux in 1864 in retaliation for their bloody uprising against the Minnesota settlements. In July 1864, Sully's force established Fort Rice on the Missouri River south of Bismarck. It then marched west accompanied by a long wagon train of men, women, and children bound for the gold fields of Montana and Idaho. Sully learned that the Sioux were encamped above the mouth of the Little Missouri at a favorite hunting ground in the Killdeer Mountains. His troops attacked the Indians there, dispersing them and destroying their camp and supplies.

The expedition resumed its westward march to the edge of the Badlands, and very likely camped in what is now the southeast corner of the park. Here, according to legend, Sully stated that the Badlands looked like "hell with the fires out." In his official report Sully described the country as "grand, dismal and majestic." From the time it arrived at the Little Missouri River until it left the Badlands, Sully's force was subjected to intermittent Sioux attacks. The expedition eventually reached the Yellowstone River, and descended it and the Missouri to Fort Berthold before returning to Fort Rice.

The Coming of the Railroad

While Sully was campaigning across the Dakota plains, railroad interests were formulating a plan to link the Great Lakes and Puget Sound. In July 1864, Congress passed the Northern Pacific Railroad Act. Already the miner with his pan and gun had caused uneasiness among the Indians. It was not long before the Sioux attacked the railroad surveyor with his compass and chain. After witnessing the decimation of the buffalo, which accompanied the construction and completion of the railroads farther south, the Indians were determined to prevent the advance of the Northern Pacific rail line west of the Missouri River. This made it necessary for the military to escort each railroad survey party.

"Hell with the fires out," where General Alfred Sully first saw the Little Missouri Badlands; Painted Canyon, Theodore Roosevelt National Park.
Theodore Roosevelt Nature & History Association/Sandra Swanson

In 1871, Maj. Joseph N. Whistler furnished an escort for a survey party which followed General Sully's route through the Badlands to the Yellowstone River. The following year, in an attempt to avoid the Badlands, Col. David S. Stanley's troops escorted a survey party south of the "oxbow" of the Little Missouri River and about 25 miles south of Whistler's survey. They continued almost straight west to the mouth of Powder River (near Terry, Montana). There they awaited the arrival of Col. Eugene M. Baker who was to escort another party of railroad surveyors east from Bozeman, Montana, to the Powder River. Sioux Indian attacks, however, led by Chief Sitting Bull and Chief Gall, forced Baker's command to abandon the survey west of Pompey's Pillar, Montana. The 1872 survey disclosed that the southerly route was not as satisfactory as Whistler's 1871 route near what is now the south boundary of the park.

Lt. Col. George A. Custer and the Seventh Cavalry accompanied Stanley's 1873 survey from Fort Abraham Lincoln near Bismarck. There were no Indian attacks until the expedition was north of present Miles City, Montana. There a major engagement between Sitting Bull's Sioux and Custer's Seventh Cavalry took place. After the survey had been completed, however, financial problems and further Indian hostility delayed construction of the railroad west from Bismarck.

Northern Pacific Railroad construction west of Bismarck, ND, 1879.
H-00228, Montana Historical Society Research Center Photograph Archives, Helena, MT

During part of the autumn and winter of 1875-76, Sitting Bull's band of about 500 lodges camped in the Badlands, apparently at the junction of Beaver Creek and the Little Missouri River. (This site is about 10 miles north of and downstream from Roosevelt's Elkhorn Ranch.)

When Custer passed through the Badlands in 1876 en route to the Battle of the Little Bighorn, his regiment camped about 5 miles south of where the town of Medora was soon to be built, on the site of the present Custer Trail Ranch. While there, Custer led a scouting party 50 miles along the Little Missouri in search of Sitting Bull's camp, but found no Indians. A blizzard on June 1 and 2 forced the regiment to camp in the badlands north of Flat Top Butte about 8 miles west of the present Custer Trail Ranch. From this camp the expedition marched up the Yellowstone River Valley to the mouth of Rosebud Creek. After a conference there with Brig. Gen. Alfred H. Terry and

Col. John Gibbon, Custer led the Seventh Cavalry northward to its fatal encounter with the Sioux.

Later in 1876, Brig. Gen. George Crook's force pursued some of the Sioux that had participated in the Custer fight. These Indians moved from the Little Bighorn to the Little Missouri and then east along what is now the south boundary of the park. When they came to the plains region east of the Badlands, they turned south. Continuing the pursuit, Crook caught up with the Indians north of the Black Hills; there he fought and beat them in the battle known as Slim Buttes.

Except for sporadic attacks, Sioux resistance had been broken by 1879, and the Northern Pacific Railroad began laying rails west from Bismarck. Late in 1879 the railroad track-laying headquarters was located on the west bank of the Little Missouri River.

In November 1879, to protect the railroad construction workers, a company of the Sixth Infantry, commanded by Capt. Stephen Baker, constructed there a military post which became known as the Badlands Cantonment. The cantonment was located about three-quarters of a mile northwest of, and across the Little Missouri River from, the present village of Medora. The sutler's store at the cantonment served as a clubhouse for the post and the surrounding region. Frank Moore served as sutler or post trader. The Badlands Cantonment was a one-company post, and only about 50 men were stationed there.

Badlands Cantonment, 1880.
H-00305, Montana Historical Society Research Center Photograph Archives, Helena, MT

The Open Range Cattle Industry

As a result of the Indian wars in the 1870's, the power of the Plains Indians was broken and the tribes placed on greatly reduced reservations. This, and the advent of the railroad on the central plains, had a direct effect on the cattle industry in Texas. There, the knowledge that the northern plains were now open to cattle raising without fear of Indian depredations, and that there were railheads connecting with the cattle markets in the East, led to the growth and expansion northward of the open range cattle industry.

This industry had its origin on the Texas plains before the Civil War. During that war the cattle had multiplied by the thousands. Soldiers, returning from the war, found the ranges covered with stock for which there was no market, and therefore selling for about a dollar a head. But the succulent grasses of the plains, and the northern railheads of the Dakota Territory opened a vista of rich profits, and the great cattle drives to the north were organized. Thousands of longhorns were driven over the Chisholm, Western, and other well-known trails. Famous cowtowns along the way, such as Newton, Wichita, Abilene, Ellsworth, and Ogallala, became shipping points to the eastern markets for Texas cattle.

The open range cattle industry was given another boost when miners and settlers poured into the Dakota Territory after the discovery of

Shipping Buffalo Hides, Dickinson, ND.
State Historical Society of North Dakota, 00739-v0002-p09e

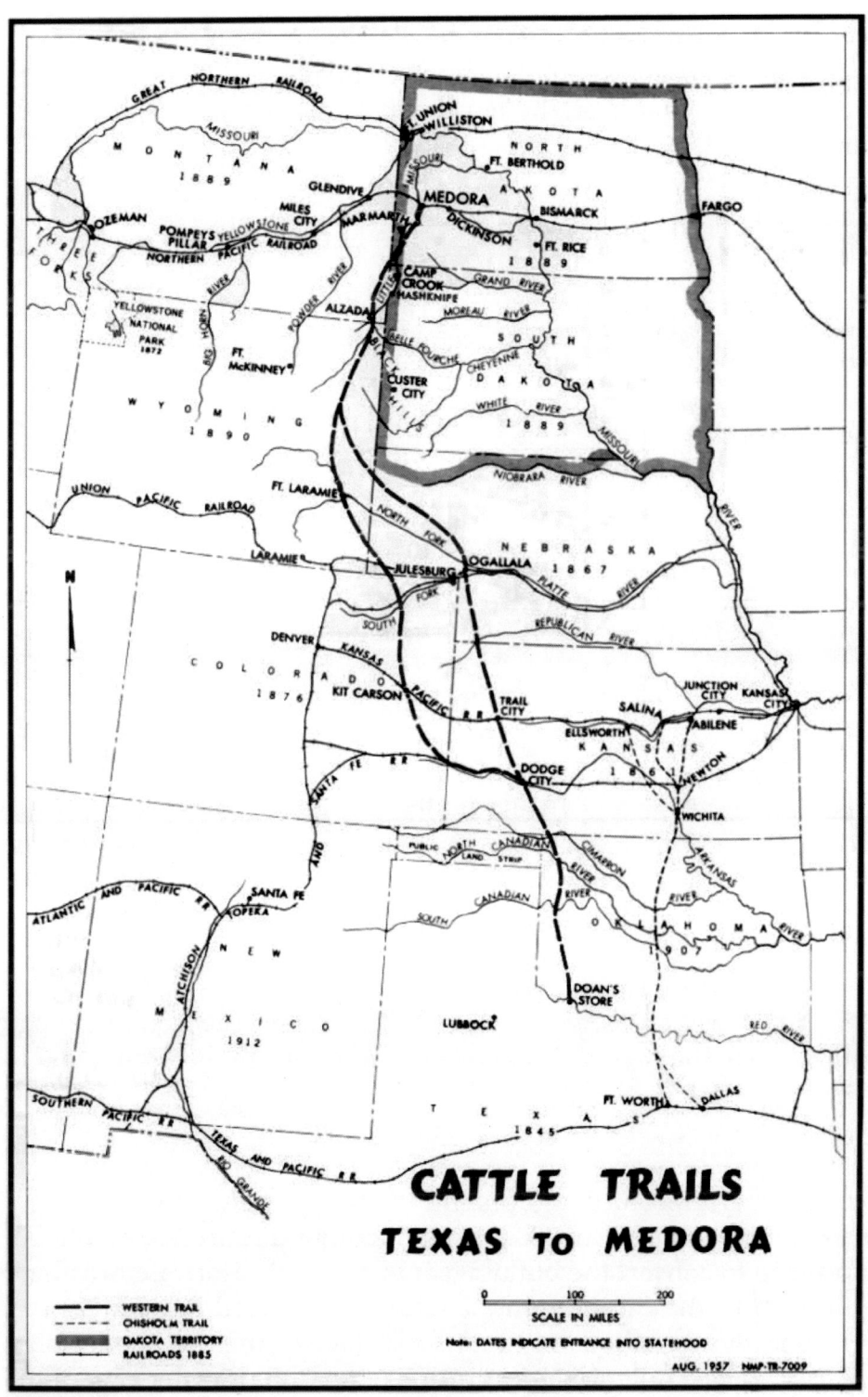

Cattle Trails
National Park Service

gold in paying quantities in the Black Hills. At about this same time, the industry was also helped by the hide hunters who were killing off the buffalo herds on the northern plains, leaving the grasslands for more cattle.

Town of Little Missouri

Pyramid Park Hotel and Depot
State Historical Society of North Dakota, 00119-00017

The early surveying parties, soldiers, and construction workers noted the abundance of wildlife in the Little Missouri Badlands. No sooner had the Northern Pacific Railway reached the Little Missouri River in September 1880 than the exploitation of the region as a game country began. Frank Moore's Pyramid Park Hotel, completed near the Badlands Cantonment in the same year, served as an outfitting point for hunting parties. Newspapers in Dakota publicized the country as a hunters' paradise. The *Bismarck Tribune* in February 1880 claimed that 2 hunters in 6 weeks' time killed 90 deer and antelope and 15 elk. It alleged that they shot 11 of the elk in about 15 minutes. Other Dakota newspapers made similar claims. E. G. Paddock and Howard Eaton, professional guides for hunting groups, ran a continuous advertisement in the Mandan Pioneer.

The Northern Pacific cooperated in publicizing the region through its tourist brochures. In them, the railroad endeavored to change the name of the region along its right-of-way from the "Badlands" to "Pyramid Park."

The publicity given the region by the railroad and newspapers was soon to affect its development. When the Badlands Cantonment was abandoned early in 1883, E. G. Gorringe, a retired naval officer, arranged to convert the buildings into a tourist resort. Before abandonment of the cantonment, a settlement named Little Missouri, and commonly called "Little Misery," had sprung up about half a mile southeast of it on the western bank of the river. In spite of the fact that Little Missouri soon earned a reputation for being a "wide open town," the excellent hunting in the vicinity attracted a number of easterners and foreigners, among them the Marquis de Mores, Howard and Alton Eaton, A. C. Huidekoper, and Theodore Roosevelt. Some of these people thought the region had potentialities as a cattle country and invested heavily in the livestock business.

Many Texas cattlemen also became interested in the northern ranges where the nutritious grasses fattened cattle more easily than the grasslands of the southern plains. Several Texas outfits developed ranches on the upper part of the Little Missouri River in present South Dakota and Montana. About this time, a Minnesota outfit, Wadsworth and Hawley, occupied a site on the Little Missouri about 15 miles north of the new settlement of "Little Misery." And about the same time Howard Eaton and E. G. Paddock established a ranch 5 miles south of the new town.

Settlement of Little Missouri, commonly known as "Little Misery".
H-00301, Montana Historical Society Research Center Photograph Archives, Helena, MT

By the end of 1883 there were a number of outfits along the Little Missouri which were largely financed by Texas, eastern, or foreign capital. Among these were the OX Ranch, near present Marmarth; the Berry, Boice Cattle Company, known as the "Three Sevens" (777); and the Continental Land and Cattle Company, commonly called the

"Hashknife." All three were Texas firms. Others were the Neimmela Ranch, financed by Sir John Pender of London; the Custer Trail Ranch, owned by a Pennsylvania family; and the Marquis de Mores operations, which had the financial backing of both eastern and foreign capital.

Little Missouri and Medora

Optimistic prospects for the Badlands were reflected in the growth of the hamlet of Little Missouri. The *Dickinson Press* described this village in September 1883 as follows:

> *This town, situated in Pyramid Park on the banks of the Little Missouri river, and surrounded by the Bad Lands with their fine scenery is, at the present time one of the most prosperous and rapidly growing towns along the line of the Northern Pacific. New buildings of every description are going up as fast as a large force of carpenters can do the work and an air of business and enterprise is apparent that would do honor to an older town... Game of all kinds is plentiful in the surrounding country and it is becoming quite a resort for pleasure seekers and those who love the chase. The country is well adapted to stock raising and Little Missouri will soon become the center of a large and growing stock interest. Marquis de Mores and C. E. Haupt are the head of Northern Pacific Refrigerator Car Company and have built a large slaughter house with capacity for slaughtering and preparing two hundred beeves daily for the market...*

Only a few months previously the Marquis de Mores had established the town of Medora opposite Little Missouri on the east bank of the river, which he named for his wife. Medora, which became the center of the Marquis' operations, was soon to overshadow in importance the older town.

Early in 1884, in the new settlement of Medora, Arthur Packard, a graduate of the University of Michigan, started a newspaper called the *Bad Lands Cow Boy*.

Lawlessness in the Little Missouri Region

Like many frontier communities, Billings County, in which both Medora and Little Missouri were located, was slow to organize its government. It early needed an effective local government to enforce law and order. The county at this time was attached to Stark County for administrative purposes and it was necessary to take violators to Dickinson, some 40 miles distant, to try them in the county courts. This difficulty no doubt contributed to the lawlessness which flourished in both Little Missouri and Medora. In January 1884 the *Glendive Times* commented on the situation:

> Little Missouri is fast gaining a very unenviable reputation. It seems as though what little law does exist in the place cannot be enforced, and the better class of citizens being in the minority a committee of safety is out of the question . . .

The *Bad Lands Cow Boy*, February 21, 1884.
Chronicling America: Historic American Newspapers. Library of Congress.

Several months later an effort was made to organize Billings County. The *Dickinson Press* gave the movement its editorial support, commenting:

> *Medora is clamoring for a county organization. We hope they will get it. If there is any place along the line that needs a criminal court and jail it is Medora. Four-fifths of the business before our justice of peace comes from Billings County.*

For some time, rustlers had been active in eastern Montana and along the Little Missouri. During the autumn and winter of 1883-84, theft, or rustling, of horses and cattle increased. The rustlers' hide-outs were hard to find and, once found, their cabins were miniature fortresses. In the spring of 1884 several individuals took the matter before the regular meeting of the Montana Stockgrowers Association in Miles City. The stockmen decided that the association itself should take no action. As a consequence, the rustlers became bolder. In July the *Bad Lands Cow Boy* summarized the situation:

> *From all parts of Dakota and Montana came reports of depredations of horse-thieves... Several men have been hung for horse-stealing, but the plague still goes on. We wish to be placed on record as believing that the only way to cure horse-stealing is to hang the thief wherever caught...*

Office of the *Bad Lands Cow Boy*.
Theodore Roosevelt Collection, Houghton Library, Harvard University

To combat the rustlers, several prominent Montana cattlemen during the summer of 1884 banded together as vigilantes. They raided eastern Montana in the late summer, and during early autumn they invaded the Little Missouri region. They hanged a number of suspicious characters, and in some instances intimidated innocent men.

While their methods may be deplored, they did discourage horse and cattle stealing. The *Cow Boy* in the following year reluctantly admitted, "the result of their work has been very wholesome" as "not a definite case of horse stealing from a cowman has been reported since." In all probability Roosevelt, as a newcomer to the region, had no part in the activities of the vigilantes. It is unlikely that he would have been invited to join an organization which depended upon secrecy for success in administering its self-appointed horse law enforcement.

Roosevelt the Buffalo Hunter

Roosevelt's avowed reason for coming to the Badlands was to hunt buffalo and other big game. He arrived there on the morning of September 7, 1883, at the depot of Little Missouri in predawn darkness. After spending a night in Little Missouri's Pyramid Park Hotel, Roosevelt met Joe Ferris near the cantonment buildings. Ferris agreed to act as Roosevelt's guide and the two set off for the Maltese Cross Ranch. Five miles south of Little Missouri they passed near Howard Eaton's Custer Trail Ranch which was later to develop into one of the first dude ranches in the United States. After fording the river twice, they came to the Maltese Cross ranchhouse about 3 miles south of Howard Eaton's place. Here Roosevelt met William Merrifield and Sylvane Ferris, Joe's brother. Roosevelt spent the night in the crude log cabin. The next day the three men continued south along the river to Gregor Lang's place at the mouth of Little Cannonball Creek near the scoria hills 50 miles south of Medora. Lang and his son Lincoln had arrived there from Scotland that spring to operate the Neimmela Ranch for Sir John Pender.

Joe Ferris
Theodore Roosevelt Birthplace NHS, Courtesy of the Theodore Roosevelt Center at Dickinson State University

Gregor Lang
Theodore Roosevelt Collection, Houghton Library, Harvard University

While utilizing the ranch as headquarters for his buffalo hunt, Roosevelt spent several evenings with Gregor Lang discussing politics and prospects for the cattle industry in the Badlands. Meanwhile, his search for buffalo was beset with many disappointments. After a week of hunting in almost continuous rains, Roosevelt and Joe Ferris discovered fresh buffalo tracks which they followed through the rough Badlands. Finally they came upon an old buffalo bull which galloped speedily away. Several miles of hard riding in pursuit brought them out of the Badlands onto the prairie. In the afternoon they sighted three old bulls, and dismounted. Roosevelt crept to within 150 feet of one of them and fired. Although he hit the buffalo, it raced off seemingly uninjured. The chase continued for another 7 or 8 miles when they finally overtook the bull. Rough ground and the speed at which they were riding caused Roosevelt to miss a shot from close range, and the animal got away.

The discouraged hunters camped for the night. The next morning, they renewed the hunt and soon sighted several buffalo. Because of rain and cold, Roosevelt missed again and the whole group thundered away. The two men spent another rainy, miserable night on the prairie. But Roosevelt continued doggedly in the hunt and shortly after noon of the third day the hunters again came upon buffalo tracks. Roosevelt approached within 50 yards of a large bull and, before the animal disappeared over a ridge, poured three shots into him. The young hunter could scarcely contain his joy when he found the bull dead in the next gully.

Not far from where Roosevelt hunted, the only sizable buffalo herd then left in the world was making its last stand. At the begnning of 1883 about 10,000 buffalo ranged south of Dickinson near the Rainy Buttes and the headwaters of the Moreau and Grand Rivers. As the year progressed, slaughter by white hide hunters reduced the herd to about 1,200. At that point James McLaughlin, superintendent of the Standing Rock Indian Agency, authorized the Sioux Indians under his authority to participate in the hunt. Between September 14 and October 23, 1883, most of the remaining buffalo were quickly killed.

The town of Sully Springs (2 miles from the South Unit of the park) was one of the most important shipping points for hides on the line of the Northern Pacific Railroad. One of the last shipments of buffalo hides on the Northern Pacific was from Dickinson in 1884. That year about 250 buffalo were sighted 7 miles south of Medora. Soon only bleaching bones were left on the prairie. For several years these towns did a thriving business in buffalo bones which were shipped east to be converted into fertilizer. As the great buffalo herds were destroyed, domestic cattle began to take their place on the vast open range.

The North Room at Sagamore Hill NHS (Roosevelt's home in Long Island, NY) showcases the bison head from Roosevelt's 1883 hunt in Dakota Territory.
Library of Congress, LC-DIG-ppmsca-36297

Roosevelt Buys a Cattle Ranch

During his buffalo hunting expedition Roosevelt had spent several evenings with Gregor Lang discussing future prospects for the cattle industry in the Badlands. One evening in the course of their conversation Roosevelt asked Lang if he would join him in a ranching venture and manage the cattle he would purchase. Being himself fully involved with Sir John Pender's cattle interests, Lang suggested Sylvane Ferris and William Merrifield who operated the Maltese Cross Ranch for Wadsworth and Hawley.

Acting upon this suggestion, Roosevelt, before returning to New York, entered into an agreement with Ferris and Merrifield and bought out the interests of Hawley and Wadsworth. According to his contract, signed at St. Paul on September 27, 1883, Roosevelt agreed to place some 400 cattle on the Chimney Butte, or Maltese Cross, Ranch at a cost of not more than $12,000. Ferris and Merrifield agreed to take care of the cattle for a 7-year period, at the end of which time 400 cattle, or their equivalent in value, were to be returned to Roosevelt and the foremen were to receive half the increase. Roosevelt was entitled by the contract to put in additional cattle on the same terms as the original 400.

Returning to New York, he was elected in November 1883, to the State Assembly, and played a part in most of the major legislation of the State for that session. However, during 1884, personal tragedy struck. Within a single night in February, both his wife and mother died. He decided that he would occupy himself by investing further in the cattle business.

Sylvane Ferris
Theodore Roosevelt Birthplace NHS, Courtesy of the Theodore Roosevelt Center at Dickinson State University

A.W. Merrifield
Theodore Roosevelt Collection, Houghton Library, Harvard University

In the months that followed, Roosevelt decided that if his cattle wintered well in the Badlands, he would start another ranch. Following the Republican National Convention in Chicago, which he attended as a delegate, Roosevelt took a train to Medora in June 1884.

On his arrival he found that the two towns on the Little Missouri had grown considerably since his previous visit some 8 months before. Medora, about a year old, was thriving. The *Mandan Pioneer* asserted early in 1884 that between February 1883 and the end of the year the 2 towns had grown from 4 buildings to 84. These included 3 hotels, 2 groceries, 2 general stores, a drygoods store, a newspaper office, a photography gallery, a blacksmith shop, a freight outfitting house, a laundry, a barber shop, and at least 5 saloons.

Sylvane Ferris and an unidentified man on horseback in front of Roosevelt's Maltese Cross Cabin, 1883.
Theodore Roosevelt Collection, Houghton Library, Harvard University

The Medora boom continued throughout 1884 and 1885. By the end of 1884 the town had 251 residents. In addition, there was a floating population estimated to number between 50 and 100 men. The *Cow Boy* boasted that Medora had "a larger freight, express and passenger business than any point on the Northern Pacific division,

Mandan and Glendive included." Several buildings erected during that period, including St. Mary's Catholic Church, the old Von Hoffman house, the old Joe Ferris store, and the present Rough Rider's Hotel, have survived. Much of Medora's prosperity, however, was due to the Marquis de Mores' packing plant and other enterprises.

In common with many of the frontier newspapers of the period, the *Bad Lands Cow Boy* was an outspoken champion of law and order and promoted the region in which it was located. Throughout 1884 and 1885, its owner continued to proclaim the Little Missouri as the "best cattle country in the world" and urged cattlemen to come there. He was also a strong supporter of the stockmen's organizations in eastern Montana and western Dakota.

Medora Railroad Station, 1886.
981-395, Montana Historical Society Research Center Photograph Archives, Helena, MT

A Typical Cattle Drive

It may be of interest to recount at this point some of the salient facts about a typical cattle drive from Texas to the northern ranges in the 1880's, a development that brought Montana and the Dakotas into prominence as a cattle range land. In 1884 Ben Bird, who was to become a contemporary of Roosevelt's in the Badlands, started from what is now Lubbock, Tex., and drove cattle to Doan's Store, a trail store at the crossing of the Red River on the Fort Griffin-Fort Dodge cattle trail. Eight or nine herds were delayed there by high water. While they waited, inspectors of the Texas Stock Growers' Association cut the trail herds-that is, they checked the brands and removed the strays so that cattle which did not rightfully belong to the trail herd would not leave Texas. When the Red River was low enough, the herd swam across.

The herd grazed northward, crossing the South and North Canadian and Arkansas Rivers. The trail then made a quarter circle west and north to avoid the settlers who were spreading west from Dodge City. The towns of Trail City, Kit Carson, and Julesburg were on the route through Colorado. At old Stoneville (Alzada), Montana, the trail divided. If the herd was driven toward Miles City it crossed the Little Missouri River there or farther north near Camp Crook. Four thousand head of Long X cattle came this way in 1884 and passed near Mingusville (Wibaux), Montana, en route to ranch headquarters (just above the present North Unit of the park). Cattle destined for ranches east of the Little Missouri were separated from the trail herd at Stoneville and followed the divide east of the river.

On the long drive north from Texas the cattle were placed on a bed ground at night. Two riders circled the herd in opposite directions so that they met twice on the way around. The herd was taken off the bed ground at daylight and grazed 2 or 3 miles along the trail before the night men were relieved for breakfast. The relief men kept the herd moving slowly along. Three thousand cattle would string out in an irregular column for a mile to a mile and a half. About 11 a. m. the lead cattle were driven off the trail and grazed until the rest of the herd caught up. About 1 p. m. the herd was started on the trail again. Generally, the cattle driven to the northern ranges were 1 or 2-year-olds.

Although methods of handling cattle were quite similar on northern and southern ranges the different purposes of the stockmen in the two sections brought about a recognizable difference. In Texas, greater emphasis was placed on breeding to produce a sizable calf crop which might eventually be sold in the north. On the northern ranges the object was to fatten the raw-boned cattle for the market as soon as possible.

Maltese Cross chuck wagon, 1884.
Theodore Roosevelt Collection, Houghton Library, Harvard University

Usually in driving the herd north the trail drivers preferred to avoid the settlements. When the herd arrived at its destination the cowboys might let go more than usual. Normally they were hardworking men and a very important cog in a highly specialized industry. In 1884 Theodore Roosevelt stated:

> The cowboys are a much misrepresented set of people. It is a popular impression that when one goes among them he must be prepared to shoot. But this is a false idea. I have taken part with them in the rounding up, have eaten, slept, hunted and herded cattle with them, and have never had any difficulty. If you choose to enter rum shops with them or go on drinking sprees with them it is as easy to get into a difficulty out there as it would be in New York, or anywhere else. But if a man minds his own business and at the same time shows that he is fully prepared to assert his rights-if he is neither a bully nor a coward and keeps out of places in which he has no business to be-he will get along as well as in Fifth Avenue. I have found them a most brave, and hospitable set of men. There is no use in trying to be overbearing with them for they won't stand the least assumption of superiority, yet there are many places in our cities where I should feel less safe than I would among the wildest cowboys of the West.

Roosevelt the Rancher

Soon after Roosevelt returned to his Maltese Cross Ranch in 1884 he began planning to extend his ranching operations. He wrote his sister, Mrs. Anna Cowles:

> ... For every day I have been here I have had my hands full. First and foremost, the cattle have done well, and I regard the outlook for making the business a success as being very hopeful. This winter I lost about 25 head from wolves, cold, etc., the others are in admirable shape, and I have about a hundred and fifty-five calves. I shall put on a thousand more cattle and shall make it my regular business. In the autumn I shall bring out Sewell and Dow and put them on a ranch with very few cattle to start with, and in the course of a couple of years give them quite a little herd also.

Acting on this decision, Roosevelt sent his ranch foremen, Sylvane Ferris and William Merrifield, to Iowa to purchase 1,000 cattle. In mid-June the *Cow Boy* noted Roosevelt's expanding operations:

> Mr. Roosevelt is still at Ferris & Merrifield's ranch, hunting and playing cowboy. It seems to be more congenial work than reforming New York state politics. He is thoroughly impressed with the profit of raising cattle in the Bad Lands, as his vigorous backing of Ferris Bros. & Merrifield testifies.

In the summer of 1884 Roosevelt took steps to establish another ranch. He selected the site for this second ranch, which he called Elkhorn, on the Little Missouri River about 35 miles north of Medora. (In common with most of the ranches of that period, both the Elkhorn and Maltese Cross were on railroad or Government land, so Roosevelt did not obtain title to either of them.) He induced two former Maine guides, Wilmot Dow and William Sewall, to become foremen of the new ranch. By August, his cattle numbered about 1,600 head. The Elkhorn buildings, begun in the autumn and winter of 1884-85, were completed in the early summer of 1885. The Elkhorn Ranch house was one of the finest in the Badlands. Roosevelt described it as the "Home Ranch House." Henceforth he spent most of his time in the Badlands there instead of at Maltese Cross.

Wilmot Dow, Theodore Roosevelt, & Bill Sewall at Elkhorn Ranch, 1886.
Theodore Roosevelt Collection, Houghton Library, Harvard University

After returning to the Badlands in the spring of 1885, Roosevelt took part in the roundup for Little Missouri District 6. Such roundup districts, as a rule, conformed to the drainage basin. These roundups were necessary because of the nature of the open range cattle industry.

Very few ranchers owned more than a section or two of land and many, including Roosevelt, were squatters owning no land whatsoever. Each rancher claimed a certain area as his range according to the number of cattle he possessed and his priority of use. The ranges were not fenced, and cattle from different ranches intermingled. Two general roundups were held each year to gather together the cattle from the range and separate them according to ownership. The spring roundup was chiefly concerned with branding calves from that year and any yearlings that had escaped branding the previous year. Cattle were handled more gently during the second, the beef, roundup in the autumn. Marketable cattle were driven to Mingusville (Wibaux), Dickinson, or Medora for shipment, or for slaughter at the De Mores packing plant in Medora.

Elkhorn Ranch House, 1886.
Theodore Roosevelt Birthplace NHS, Courtesy of the Theodore Roosevelt Center at Dickinson State University

    The roundup started from the mouth of Box Elder Creek on the Little Missouri. The men worked down the river to Big Beaver and up that stream until they made a juncture with men from the Yellowstone roundup. Cattle ranging within 40 miles east of the Little Missouri were driven to that river before the general roundup. It was usually necessary for each ranch to have representatives in adjacent roundup districts in addition to its own. The cook drove his outfit's wagon with bedding, food, and other provisions for the men. About 50 or more men were assigned to a district. Each cowboy had a string of 8 or 10 horses.

On a typical day's roundup one or two men would start from the head of each stream or draw in the district to be covered, driving the cattle ahead of them to a point of concentration which might be a wide bottomland near the river, like Beef Corral Bottom. Cutting the herd (separation of cattle according to brands) usually took place at the point of concentration. Both horse and rider had to be well trained to cut individual cattle from a restless herd of several thousand. Cutting was not a job for greenhorns or dudes.

Elkhorn Ranch Stable.
Theodore Roosevelt Collection, Houghton Library, Harvard University

Like the long drive from Texas, the roundup required a well-trained team. In contrast to the long drive it was desirable to end the roundup as soon as possible without being too hard on the horses they rode or the cattle they drove. Only the most experienced men were assigned to the various tasks. Roosevelt never claimed to be a good roper or more than an average rider by ranch standards. Accordingly, while on the roundup he was not assigned the important tasks of cutting, roping, or branding. In the spring roundups, however, he provided fresh meat for the cowboys by hunting.

At the time of the spring roundup of 1885, Roosevelt apparently added more cattle to both of his herds. A contemporary news item stated:

> Fifteen hundred head of steers, yearlings and two's came in Thursday morning for the Elkhorn and Chimney Butte ranches of Theodore Roosevelt. They were in fair condition after their long ride and except for the disadvantage of a large number being yearlings, give every evidence of growing into good beef. The larger majority are steers. A good lot of Short-horn bulls and one Polled Angus were in the herd. A thousand of these cattle will be driven to the Elkhorn Ranch and five hundred to the already well-stocked Chimney Butte

Cattle losses were light on the northern plains during the winter of 1885-86. Unlike the region farther south, the winter in Dakota and Montana was comparatively mild. After spending that winter in New York City, Roosevelt returned to Dakota in March. Soon after his arrival he wrote Mrs. Cowles:

Things are looking better than I expected; the loss by cattle has been trifling. Unless we have a big accident I shall get through this all right. If not I can get started with no debt.

A letter written about 3 months later to his brother-in-law, Douglas Robinson, expressed similar sentiments:

... While I do not see any very great fortune ahead yet if things go on as they are now going and have gone for the past three years I think I will each year net enough money to pay a good interest on the capital, and yet be adding slowly to my herd all the time. I think I have more than my original capital on the ground, and this year I ought to be able to sell between two and three hundred head of steers and drystock.

Elkhorn Ranch house opposite the Little Missouri River (photograph taken by Theodore Roosevelt), 1886.
Theodore Roosevelt Collection, Houghton Library, Harvard University

During 1885-86, Roosevelt's ranching operations were at their peak. Unfortunately, there is no information other than that provided by the tax records of Billings and Stark Counties and the census records to show just how many cattle he owned outright at any time. The estimates vary from about 3,000 to 5,000 head. He was not the biggest operator in the Badlands; neither was he one of the smallest. The census rolls for 1885 disclose that Roosevelt was the fourth largest cattleman in Billings County, which was then of considerably larger area than at present. The census records also show that Ferris, Merrifield, and Roosevelt together owned 3,350 cattle and 1,100 calves. It is highly probable that these figures represent somewhere near the maximum number of cattle on the two Roosevelt ranches. His total investment amounted to about $82,500. Outfits such as the "Three Sevens," "Hashknife," and the "OX" ran as many as 15,000 head of cattle on the Dakota ranges.

In the Little Missouri spring roundup of 1886, Roosevelt took part as co-captain. Letters to his family indicate he spent considerable time in the saddle. On June 7 he wrote his sister:

I have been on the roundup for a fortnight and really enjoy the work greatly; in fact I am passing a most pleasant summer, though I miss all of you very, very much. We breakfast at three every morning, and work from sixteen to eighteen hours a day, counting night guard; so I get pretty sleepy; but I feel strong as a bear.

Theodore Roosevelt on the round-up, 1885.
Theodore Roosevelt Collection, Houghton Library, Harvard University

CHIMNEY BUTTE RANCH.
THEODORE ROOSEVELT, Proprietor.
FERRIS & MERRIFIELD, Managers.

P. O. address, Little Missouri, D. T. Range, Little Missouri, 8 miles south of railroad.

as in cut on left hip and right side, both or either, and down cut dewlap.

Horse brand, on left hip.

ELKHORN RANCH.
THEODORE ROOSEVELT, Proprietor.
SEAWALL & DOW, Managers.

P. O. address, Little Missouri, D. T. Range, Little Missouri, twenty-five miles north of railroad.

as in cut, on left side, on right, or the reverse. Horse brand, on right or left shoulder.

Roosevelt's Brands. From Stockgrowers Journal, Miles City, MT (Sewall's name is misspelled).
Theodore Roosevelt National Park, Courtesy of the Theodore Roosevelt Center at Dickinson State University

Roosevelt apparently spent part of his time during the roundup writing and hunting for he wrote several weeks later to his sister:

I write steadily three or four days, and then hunt (I killed two elk and some antelope recently) or ride on the roundup for many more.

One morning that spring at the Elkhorn Ranch, Roosevelt discovered that his boat had been stolen. His foremen, Sewall and Dow, immediately improvised another boat and the three started their search for the culprits. The weather was bitterly cold. At the mouth of Cherry Creek (about 12 miles east of the North Unit), Roosevelt and his foremen caught up with the three thieves, while they were encamped, got "the drop" on them, and forced the trio to surrender. For several days both captors and prisoners were unable to travel because of ice jams in the river. Roosevelt passed his idle time by reading Tolstoy's *Anna Karenina* and some of the writings of Matthew Arnold. Provisions ran short. After obtaining supplies and a wagon from the Diamond C Ranch, located several miles northwest of the present town of Killdeer, Roosevelt took the prisoners by wagon to Dickinson and turned them over to the sheriff. Meanwhile, his foremen in the recovered boat descended the Little Missouri and Missouri Rivers to Mandan, from which point they shipped the boat by rail to Medora. The 3 thieves were tried in Mandan the following August and 2 were sent to the penitentiary.

T.R. Guarding the Boat Thieves. Staged image of the capture of three thieves who stole Roosevelt's boat. Sewall, Dow, and unidentified man pose as thieves.
Theodore Roosevelt Collection Houghton Library, Harvard University

That summer Roosevelt was one of the featured speakers at the Fourth of July celebration in Dickinson. His address received favorable comment in the *Dickinson Press* and other Dakota newspapers. While he was at the Maltese Cross, and during the intervals he was in New York, Roosevelt completed writing his *Hunting Trips of a Ranchman* as well as several articles for *Outlook* and *Century* magazines. A good part of his *Life of Thomas Hart Benton* was written at the Elkhorn Ranch. Later, he wrote *The Winning of the West*, undoubtedly drawing on his Badland's experiences for his understanding of pioneer conditions. The bookshelves at the Elkhorn Ranch reflected his naturalist and historical interests. Included among the books to be found there were Elliot Coues' *Birds of the Northwest* and Col. Richard Dodge's *Plains of the Great West*. The works of Irving, Hawthorne, Cooper, and Lowell were represented, and there was also lighter reading. Often when hunting or on the roundup, he carried a book in his saddle pack. Such cultural interests and attainments, needless to relate, were quite a rarity on the cattlemen's frontier.

Roosevelt and the Marquis de Mores

Much has been written about Roosevelt's relations with the Marquis de Mores. A few writers have claimed that the two men were generally unfriendly and at one time were on the verge of fighting a duel.

Several months before Roosevelt first came to the Badlands, the life of De Mores reportedly was threatened by a trio of hunters, including a man named Riley Luffsey. The Marquis and several of his men were involved in a gunfight in which Luffsey was killed. In a trial held July 1883 the Marquis and other defendants were acquitted. But in 1885 another indictment was brought against them for the murder of Luffsey.

At the time of the second trial several men who were testifying against De Mores obtained money from Ferris who served as banker for a few of the local cowboys. Because Ferris was regarded as Roosevelt's man, it appeared to the Marquis that Roosevelt must be behind the opposition to him. At this time several newspapers published accounts of an alleged quarrel between Roosevelt and De Mores. One paper stated that the main reason for their antagonism was that they were like "two very big toads in a very small puddle." While the Marquis was in jail in connection with this second trial (he was again acquitted), and under a serious mental strain, he wrote the following letter to Roosevelt, which has been interpreted by some as a challenge to a duel:

Bismark, Dak., Sept 3 1885

My dear Roosevelt
My principle is to take the bull by the horns. Joe Ferris is very active against me and has been instrumental in getting me indicted by furnishing money to witnesses and hunting them up. The papers also publish very stupid accounts of our quarelling- I sent you the paper to N. Y. Is this done by your orders. I thought you my friend. If you are my enemy I want to know it. I am always on hand as you know, and between gentlemen it is easy to settle matters of that sort directly.

Marquis de Morès on Horseback, 1886.
State Historical Society of North Dakota, 0042-078

Yours very truly,
Mores.

I hear the people want to organize the county. I am opposed to it for one year more at least.

An undated draft of Roosevelt's reply follows:

Most emphatically I am not your enemy; if I were you would know it, for I would be an open one, and would not have asked you to my house nor gone to yours. As your final words however seem to imply a threat it is due to myself to say that the statement is not made through any fear of possible consequences to me; I too, as you know, am always on hand, and ever ready to hold myself accountable in any way for anything I have said or done.

Yours very truly,
Theodore Roosevelt.

This exchange of correspondence apparently ended the incident. Except for this incident, Roosevelt's relations with De Mores, so far as is known, were amicable. On several occasions he visited the Marquis and Marquise at their "chateau" overlooking the Little Missouri.

The Stockmen's Association

For some time a number of Little Missouri ranchers had recognized a need for a stockmen's organization to enforce range rules. Early in 1884, Howard Eaton and several others had initiated such a movement. The *Bad Lands Cow Boy* supported their efforts and editorialized:

> *We are glad to see that Mr. Howard Eaton has taken the initiative in the one thing that is now most important to our cattle men. We refer to the subject of a cattle organization... This is a matter of vital interest to every stock man of the Bad Lands. Subjects continually come up that should be settled by a vote of the majority of our cattle men. At present there is no organization and each man must decide all questions for himself. ...*

Howard Eaton
Theodore Roosevelt National Park, Courtesy of the Theodore Roosevelt Center at Dickinson State University

In February the stockmen had held a meeting in Little Missouri and appointed a committee to draw up bylaws for a formal organization. However, in the next meeting, the ranchers decided to defer the matter. But Roosevelt lent his support to the movement and took the initiative in bringing together the scattered stockmen along the Little Missouri for that purpose. He visited the ranchers along the river and convinced them of the desirability of organizing. Roosevelt issued calls in the Cow Boy for a meeting of the stockmen in Medora on December 19, 1884. The proceedings of this meeting reflect Roosevelt's leadership. Representatives of the 11 cattle companies attending elected him chairman of the organization, which called itself the Little Missouri Stockmen's Association, and they drew up resolutions and rules for a permanent organization. Roosevelt was authorized to draw up the constitution and bylaws. The following week the *Cow Boy* commented:

> *The stockmen's meeting last Friday morning bids fair to be the beginning of a very efficient organization. The utmost harmony and unanimity prevailed, and under the able chairmanship of Theodore Roosevelt, a large amount of business was transacted in a short time. ...*

Roosevelt was reelected chairman in 1885 and president of the association in 1886. *The Cow Boy* again complimented him for his work as chairman:

> *The association can congratulate itself on again electing Theodore Roosevelt as president. Under his administration, everything moves quickly forward and there is none of that time-consuming, fruitless talk that so invariably characterizes a deliberative assembly without a good presiding officer.*

Roosevelt was also an active member in the Montana Stockgrowers Association, with which the Little Missouri group was affiliated. He was admitted to membership in the Montana Stockgrowers Association in April 1885 on the recommendation of De Mores; but he did not attend its annual meeting that year. In 1886 the Little Missouri association sent Roosevelt as a delegate to one of the Montana meetings. He was placed on a committee of 16 prominent stockmen of the 2 territories to investigate the feasibility of establishing stockyards and a market in St. Paul. In another act of recognition he and Henry S. Boice were named captains of the Little Missouri Roundup. Roosevelt was also selected as one of the three members of the executive committee from the Dakota Territory.

Roosevelt's role in the 1887 annual meeting was even more conspicuous. Again, he was named to the executive committee.

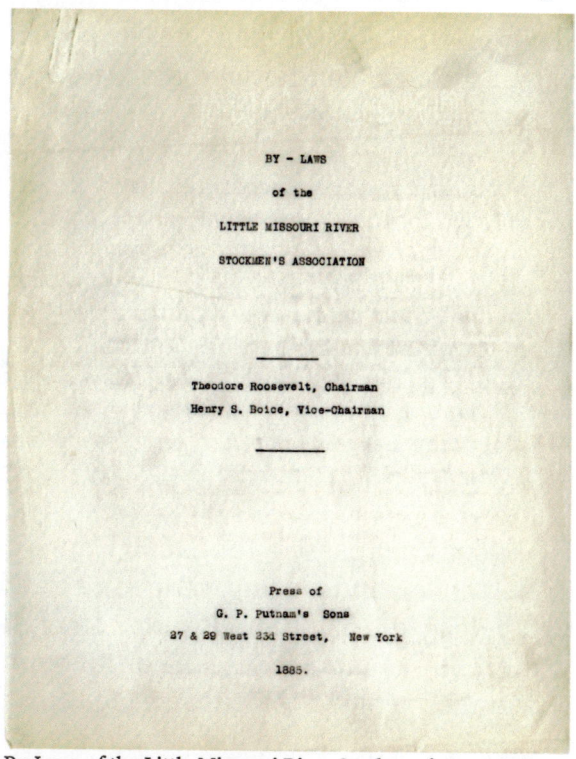

By-Laws of the Little Missouri River Stockmen's Association.
Theodore Roosevelt Center at Dickinson State University

To discourage horse stealing, he introduced a resolution to require the members of the association to keep a record of all suspicious persons visiting their ranches and the brand of such person's horses. He also preferred charges before the Board of Commissioners against livestock inspector Fred Willard and succeeded in getting him discharged. This was the last meeting of the Montana Stockgrowers Association which Roosevelt attended.

The Winter of 1886-87

Prior to 1886, nature had been kind to Roosevelt and his neighboring ranchers in the Little Missouri Badlands. Their losses during the previous winters had been relatively small. The winter of 1885-86 also was a mild one on the northern plains and there was but little snow in Dakota and Montana. On the other hand, the winter on the southern plains had been extremely severe. During the summer of 1886 cattlemen from the south continued to drive herds to the parched and already overstocked ranges of the north.

By midsummer the situation had become alarming. When Roosevelt passed through Mandan en route to New York a reporter of the *Mandan Pioneer* interviewed him:

> *A few days ago, Mr. Theodore Roosevelt passed through Mandan on his way to New York after spending four months on his ranch in the western part of the territory.... Then, speaking of the season on the ranches, he stated where they are wisely and honestly managed they are now paying fairly well but no excessive profits. The days of excessive profits are over. There are too many in the business. In certain sections of the West the losses this year are enormous, owing to the drouth and overstocking. Each steer needs from fifteen to twenty-five acres, but they are crowded on very much thicker, and the cattlemen this season have paid the penalty. Between the drouth, the grasshoppers, and the late frosts, ice forming as late as June 10, there is not a green thing in all the region he has been over. ...*

As summer passed, range conditions continued to become worse. Little rain fell and grazing was poor. Fires destroyed much of the grass that remained. The fate of many stockmen depended upon a mild winter. But as one writer said of the winter of 1886-87, "nature and economics seemed to conspire together for the entire overthrow of the [open range cattle] industry." Late in November the first severe storm struck. The *Bismarck Tribune* described it as "in many respects the worst on record." Comparatively mild weather followed during the first half of December and a part of the snow melted. Then subzero weather in late December, which lasted until mid- January, formed a crust of impenetrable ice from the melting snow. Cattle could not get through the crusted snow to the grass below. As a result, many of them perished. New heavy snows fell. During the middle of January there was thawing weather accompanied by rain. Again the soggy snow froze. Throughout the remainder of January and during most of February there was continued subzero weather and more heavy snows. Only warm chinook winds which struck in the northern plains in early March saved the stockmen from complete disaster.

The first reports of the results of the winter were quite optimistic. But it was not until after the roundups of the summer that the cattlemen were able to appraise their losses.

The winter of 1886-87 was devasting to cattle and cattlemen of the Northern Great Plains. Print by C. Graham (printed in Harper's Weekly) was based on a sketch by H. Worrall.
Library of Congress, LC-USZ62-100252 DLC

Roosevelt had returned to New York City in the late summer of 1886, and received the Republican nomination for Mayor of New York City. But in the November election he suffered a severe defeat. The next month he married Miss Edith Carow in England, and the couple spent the winter honeymooning in Europe.

Reports of the hard winter on the northern plains and the heavy losses in cattle brought Roosevelt back from Europe. He went immediately to Medora to study the situation. From there he wrote his friend, Henry Cabot Lodge, soon after his arrival:

> *Well, we have had a perfect smashup all through the cattle country of the northwest. The losses are crippling. For the first time I have been utterly unable to enjoy a visit to my ranch. I shall be glad to get home.*

He wrote his sister in a similar vein:

> *I am bluer than indigo about the cattle; it is even worse than I feared; I wish I was sure I would lose no more than half the money ($80,000) I invested out here. I am planning to get out of it.*

Roosevelt attended the spring meetings of the stockmen's association. There it was decided that, owing to the heavy losses, the Little Missouri stockmen should not hold a general roundup. Believing that the cattle had drifted with the storm, the group decided to send a party to the Standing Rock Indian Reservation in search of them.

The ranchers combed the country in vain for the cattle they believed had drifted in the winter storms. As one stockman pointed out," Search it [the range] minutely and there was no sign of the tragedy. The carcasses withered up by the end of August, a few bones grass-covered at wide intervals and that was all. How the thousands of cows and steers that died had left no trace is an enigma." By late summer of 1887, after the summer roundups, the cattlemen were able to make somewhere near accurate appraisals. The *Mandan Pioneer* estimated the losses for the northern plains at about 75 percent.

In May, Roosevelt was back in New York City. We do not know with any certainty how great his losses were from the winter of 1886-87. The Billings County tax records indicate he paid taxes on 60 percent less cattle in 1887 than in 1886.

The effects of the winter of 1886-87 were also felt in Medora. The De Mores packing plant, which had cut down operations the previous autumn because of the drought, closed for good the summer of 1887. Many of the residents of Medora and Little Missouri then moved to Dickinson. The Medora newspaper, the *Bad Lands Cow Boy*, also went out of business in 1887, after a fire destroyed the office and press. In 1889 the *Dickinson Press* reported:

> Medora had a short season of rapid growth when that charming French nobleman and rather visionary man of business, the Marquis de Mores made it the seat of his slaughtering and beef-shipping enterprise. The big abbatoir is silent and deserted now, and is presumably the property of his creditors. The brick hotel is closed and so is the Marquis' Chateau on the hill and there is small use for the brick church he built...

Medora from Railway Bridge, 1886.
981-392, Montana Historical Society Research Center Photograph Archives, Helena, MT

Marquis de Mores Packing Plant, 1886.
981-394, Montana Historical Society Research Center Photograph Archives, Helena, MT

Medora continued to decline, until it was almost a ghost town. The village of Little Missouri across the river fared worse, and eventually disappeared. The hard winter had dealt a staggering blow to the open range cattle industry in the Little Missouri Badlands. Most of the outfits which were backed by eastern or foreign capital withdrew from the business. A few managed, however, to hang on without outside financial support. Several big outfits, such as the "Three Sevens," the "Hashknife," and the Huidekopers, continued in business until the end of the century. Pierre Wibaux, unlike most of his contemporaries, bought up the remnants of many of the herds after that harsh winter. By the 1890's he had in the neighborhood of 40,000 head and was one of the largest operators in the United States.

Pierre and Nellie Wibaux
State Historical Society of North Dakota, D-0187-00001

Roosevelt's Later Ranching Operations

Following the hard winter of 1886-87, Roosevelt's trips to his Dakota ranches were less frequent. His devotion to his family and his rising political fortunes were no doubt influences that kept him in the East. Nevertheless, he continued trying for more than a decade to recoup his losses in the Badlands. Records regarding his ranching ventures, which were kept at the Elkhorn Ranch during this period, are meager and obscure. Some time between 1890 and 1892 Roosevelt abandoned the Elkhorn Ranch, shifting his activities to the Maltese Cross. The tax records indicate that his herds dwindled over a period of several years.

In 1892 Roosevelt redoubled his efforts to recoup his losses. In March of that year, together with Archibald D. Russell, R. H. M. Ferguson, and Douglas Robinson, he organized the Elkhorn Ranch Company, incorporated under the laws of New York. He transferred his cattle holdings, valued at $16,500, to this company, and later invested in it a further sum of $10,200. Sylvane Ferris served as manager of the new organization. Soon the new company began to purchase more cattle. In May 1892 the Dickinson Press reported, "Theodore Roosevelt... has 1,000 head of cattle in the Badlands out of Medora... Through Mr. Roosevelt's manager, S. M. Ferris, 300 head were purchased recently." Additional purchases were made 2 years later. Roosevelt spent short periods in the Badlands during the late summers or early autumns of 1887, 1888, 1890, 1892, 1893, and 1896. But his political success in the East during the 1890's made it increasingly difficult for him to give attention to his ranching ventures. From 1889 to 1895 he was a member of the United States Civil Service Commission. For the next 2 years he was president of the Police Commission of New York City. In 1897, President McKinley appointed him Assistant Secretary of the Navy.

By this time the number of Roosevelt's cattle had dwindled considerably, and he reached the conclusion that he should sell out. In December 1897 he wrote his foreman, Sylvane Ferris, "Evidently we must try to dispose of all the cattle on the ranch next year." In April 1898 the United States was at war with Spain. Roosevelt, who was then planning on going to Cuba as a lieutenant colonel of the cavalry that became known as the "Rough Riders," sold his cattle interest to Sylvane Ferris.

Roosevelt's losses from his ranching ventures were heavy. According to Hermann Hagedorn, his biographer, Roosevelt's initial investment in the two ranches was $82,500. Of this, he lost approximately $23,500. His investment in the Elkhorn Stock Company, however, yielded him a profit of $3,250, which reduced his net loss from his Dakota venture to about $20,000. Considering loss on interest on $82,500 at 5 percent for the period from September 1884 to February 1899, his total loss would amount to about $50,000.

Near the close of the 19th century and at the beginning of the 20th, the Government surveyed much of the Little Missouri Badlands. The region was then opened to homesteaders. About the same time the Northern Pacific Railway sold its lands in the region. These two events marked the end of the open range. As a result, most of the remaining big cattle outfits went out of the business.

The Further Career of the Marquis de Mores

Perhaps a word should be said here about the career of the Marquis de Mores after the failure of his Medora venture. Since his name is inextricably associated with the history of Medora, it is of interest to recount what eventually became of him. The story of his subsequent life is both stirring and tragic. De Mores returned to France, and then went to India for a year. Then he journeyed on to China where he toyed with plans designed to increase the influence of his native France. Returning to France he became involved in its political storms and it is alleged he took a part in the Dreyfus Affair and in trying to overthrow the government. He dreamed of augmenting the power of France in Africa, and as a means of doing so he is supposed to have conceived a plan to unite the Moslems against England. He went to Tunis in 1896 to lead an expedition into the Sudan and unite the Arabs in resisting the English advance in Africa. Against the advice of friends, he exchanged an Arab escort for one of wild Touareg tribesmen. They led him into an ambush at the well of El Ouatia. There he fell, but not until after he had left a ring of dead men around him. French colonial officials later recovered De Mores' body and returned it to Paris. He is buried there.

Roosevelt's Later Visits to Medora

When Roosevelt returned from the Cuban campaign in 1898, he found himself widely acknowledged as a national hero. In the same year he was elected Governor of New York, and in 1900 he was elected Vice President of the United States. An assassin's bullet less than a year later killed President McKinley and Roosevelt became President- the youngest man in history to assume that office. While making a tour of the West in March 1903 Roosevelt stopped in Medora where, as he described it, "the entire population of the Bad Lands down to the smallest baby had gathered to meet me." In 1911 he again made a short stop in that Badlands cowtown, and from the rear platform of his private car, shook hands with his former acquaintances.

Roosevelt visits Medora, 1903.
Library of Congress, Courtesy of Dickinson State University

Roosevelt and the Conservation Movement

As early as 1889, Maj. John Wesley Powell, "the prophet of the arid region," warned North Dakota's constitutional convention of the dangers of plowing the central and western part of the State unless irrigation water was at hand. Roosevelt also appreciated the vital need for irrigation, profiting by his ranch life in the Little Missouri Badlands and his hunting experiences throughout the West. The passing of the frontier, commonly considered to date from 1890, dramatized the need for conservation.

Early in 1901 Representative Francis G. Newlands of Nevada and Senator Henry C. Hansbrough of North Dakota introduced a reclamation bill in the Congress. In December 1901, shortly after the assassination of President McKinley, F. H. Newell, who had been one of Powell's assistants, and Gifford Pinchot, Chief of the Division of Forestry, U. S. Department of Agriculture, since 1898, met with Roosevelt and discussed plans for irrigating arid lands of the West. Roosevelt included this subject in his first message to Congress. On June 17, 1902, the "Newlands Bill" was signed by the President and became known as the Reclamation Act of 1902. This is the basic law of the Bureau of Reclamation.

Before Roosevelt had become President, he had helped to organize the Boone and Crockett Club, which was dedicated to the preservation of America's big game. One of his first acts after becoming President was to encourage the Congress to establish a new herd of buffalo in Yellowstone National Park so that they would not become extinct. Roosevelt indicated the true purpose of the national parks concept when he stated:

> *I cannot too often repeat that the essential feature in th present management of the Yellowstone Park, as in all similar places, is its essential democracy-it is the preservation of the scenery, of the forests, of the wilderness life and the wilderness game for the people as a whole ...*

Roosevelt also warned that the United States was exhausting its forest supplies more rapidly than they were being produced. His concept of his duty as President was that he should act affirmatively for the general welfare where the Constitution did not explicitly forbid him to act. Although he did not originate the ideas behind many of the conservation measures, he did furnish the necessary vigorous influence and publicity that helped push the projects through Congress.

In 1905 he created the Forest Service as a separate bureau of the Department of Agriculture. During his 7.5 years as President more than 3 times as much acreage was added to the national forests than had been reserved during all previous years. At the close of his administration 194,505,325 acres had been designated as national forests. One of the newly established areas was the Dakota National Forest on the southern extremity of the "oxbow" of the Little Missouri River.

In addition to proposals for water, forest, and mineral conservation, Roosevelt favored a change in western land policy. Major Powell had urged that the size of grazing homesteads be increased. Roosevelt supported this viewpoint, but also urged the careful examination and classification of public grazing lands in order to give each settler land enough to support his family. As President, he supported the conservation of America's scenery and natural and historic objects. Up to 1906 the prehistoric ruins of the Southwest had been subjected to extensive vandalism. Roosevelt signed the Antiquities Act of 1906, which provided that the President could set aside, for public use as national monuments, objects and landmarks of scientific and historic interest. Under its provisions President Theodore Roosevelt established the first 16 national monuments.

At the suggestion of the Inland Waterways Commission, which he had appointed in 1907, the President called for a National Conservation Congress which met the following year. This meeting was a landmark in American conservation. Besides arousing general interest in conservation at both the State and national level, it made provision for an inventory of the Nation's natural resources by the National Conservation Commission which the President appointed in 1908. Through creation of the National Conservation Commission he assured the continuity of the conservation movement.

Establishment of the Park

Early in 1919, after Roosevelt's death, a movement was initiated to establish a Roosevelt National Park in the Little Missouri Badlands. In 1921 Carl Olsen, owner of the Peaceful Valley Dude Ranch, introduced a bill in the North Dakota Legislature which petitioned the Congress of the United States to establish Roosevelt Park, but Congress did not respond favorably at that time.

Attempts had been made to farm the region since it was first opened to settlement in the early 1900's. The drought and depression of the 1930's, however, proved that the Badlands were not suitable cropland. Through the Resettlement Administration, lands which had been classified as submarginal were retired from private ownership and later were utilized for grazing under the administration of the Soil Conservation Service and local grazing associations. In the mid-1930's the Resettlement Administration began purchasing the lands now in the park. Under the technical direction and supervision of the National Park Service, and with the labor and materials supplied by various relief agencies, the park was first developed as Roosevelt Recreational Demonstration Area. In 1946 the area became Theodore Roosevelt National Wildlife Refuge. An Act of Congress on April 25, 1947, established Theodore Roosevelt National Memorial Park and returned its administration to the National Park Service. In 1978, the park's designation was officially changed to Theodore Roosevelt National Park.

Park Dedication, Theodore Roosevelt National Memorial Park, 1949.
National Park Service

Theodore Roosevelt National Park preserves 70,446 acres of land across three different units of western North Dakota (North, South, and Elkhorn Ranch Units). The scenic landscape is similar to what Roosevelt saw in the 1880's. The landscape bears more than just his name; it also bears remnants of his two former ranches. Within the park, the iconic symbols of Roosevelt's ranching days include the Maltese Cross Cabin and the Elkhorn Ranch Site. The Maltese Cross Cabin rests on National Park grounds just behind the South Unit Visitor Center in Medora. Guided tours of this ranch house are given daily throughout the summer months.

The Elkhorn Ranch Site lies within Theodore Roosevelt National Park at the Elkhorn Ranch Unit, a 218-acre site situated along the Little Missouri River. While the site is open year-round, access is limited due to its remoteness and roads. The site contains the historic grounds of Roosevelt's Elkhorn Ranch buildings, however all that remains of the structures are foundations accessible by footpath. While few of the park's visitors ever reach the Elkhorn, those who do are rewarded with many of the same experiences Theodore Roosevelt had while sitting on the front porch of his cabin staring across the "sharply channeled barren buttes." For many, these experiences present a genuine connection to Theodore Roosevelt and the Dakota Badlands.

Roosevelt's Maltese Cross Ranch Cabin, located behind the South Unit Visitor Center in Medora.
Theodore Roosevelt Nature & History Assocation/Katherine Plessner

Elkhorn Ranch Site
National Park Service/Laura Thomas